Contents

11

20

39

54

Beginner Wristers

Basic

MEASUREMENTS
Circumference Approx 7"/18cm
Length Approx 7"/18cm
Note Wristers will stretch to fit a range of sizes.

MATERIALS
Yarn
LION BRAND® *Heartland*®, *Thick & Quick*® 5oz/142g skeins; each
125yd/114m (acrylic) (6)
• 1 skein in #151 Katmai

Needles
• One pair size 11 (8mm) knitting needles, *or size to obtain gauge*

Notion
• Tapestry needle

GAUGE
11 stitches = 4"/10cm in garter st (k all sts in every row) using size
11 (8mm) needles. *BE SURE TO CHECK YOUR GAUGE.*

NOTES
1) Each Wrister is worked as a simple garter-stitch rectangle.
2) To make the Wristers, each rectangle is sewn into a tube, leaving
an opening for thumb.

WRISTERS (MAKE 2)
Cast on 19 sts.
Work in garter st until the piece measures approx 7"/18cm from the
beginning.
Bind off.

FINISHING
Cut yarn, leaving a yarn tail about 18"/45.5cm long. Thread the end of
the yarn tail into the blunt needle.
Fold the piece, bringing the cast on edge to meet the bound-off
edge.
With the threaded blunt needle, sew the edges together, leaving a
2"/5cm opening for your thumb.
Weave in the yarn ends. •

Helix Leg Warmers

Easy

MEASUREMENTS
Circumference Approx 11 1/2"/29cm at upper edge
Height Approx 26"/66cm

MATERIALS
Yarn
LION BRAND® *Mandala*®, 5.3oz/150g skeins; each 590yd/540m (acrylic) (3)
• 1 skein in #208 Valkyrie

Needles
• One set (5) double-pointed needles (dpn) size 4 (3.5mm), *or size to obtain gauge*
• One set (5) double-pointed needles (dpn) size 5 (3.75mm), *or size to obtain gauge*

Notions
• Stitch markers
• Tapestry needle

GAUGE
22 sts + 32 rnds = 4"/10cm over St st worked in rnds (k every rnd), using size 5 (3.75mm) dpn. *BE SURE TO CHECK YOUR GAUGE.*

K2, P2 RIB IN THE ROUND
(Over a multiple of 4 sts)
Rnd 1 *K2, p2; rep from * to end of rnd.
Rep Rnd 1 for K2, p2 Rib worked in rnds.

NOTES
1) Leg Warmers are knit in one piece in the round on double-pointed needles.
2) The color variations of the yarn mean your Leg Warmers will not be identical.

LEG WARMERS (MAKE 2)
With smaller needles, cast on 64 sts. Divide sts onto 4 needles with 16 sts on each needle. Pm for beg of rnd and join by working the first st on the left-hand needle with the working yarn from the right-hand needle, being careful not to twist sts.
Work in k2, p2 rib worked in the rnd until piece measures about 3"/7.5cm.

Change to larger needles and work in St st worked in rnds until piece measures approx 4½"/11.5cm from beg.
Dec Rnd K2tog, k to last 2 sts, ssk—62 sts.
Knit 11 rnds.
Rep last 12 rnds until you have 44 sts.
Continue in St st worked in the rnd until piece measures approx 23½"/59.5cm from beg.
Change to smaller needles, and work in k2, p2 rib worked in the rnd for 2½"/6.5cm.
Bind off.

FINISHING
Weave in ends. •

Simple Hat

Basic

MEASUREMENTS
Circumference Approx 18½"/47cm
Height Approx 11"/28cm
Note Hat will stretch to fit a range of sizes.

MATERIALS
Yarn
LION BRAND® *Wool-Ease®, Thick & Quick®,* 5oz/140g skeins; each
87yd/80m (acrylic, wool) (6)
• 1 skein in #610 Hudson Bay

Needles
• One set (5) double-pointed needles (dpn) size 11 (8mm, *or size to
obtain gauge*

Notions
• Stitch marker
• Tapestry needle

GAUGE
9 stitches = 4"/10cm over St st worked in the rnd (k every rnd), using
size 11 (8mm) dpn. *BE SURE TO CHECK YOUR GAUGE.*

NOTE
Hat is worked in one piece in the round on double-pointed needles
(dpn). If you prefer, you can work the hat on a 16"/40.5cm long
circular needle, then change to double-pointed needles to work
the last round.

HAT
Cast 42 sts onto 4 of the dpn—with 10 sts on each of 2 needles and
11 sts on each of 2 needles.
Place marker for the beg of the rnd. Join by working the first st on
the left-hand needle with the working yarn from the right-hand
needle and being careful not to twist the sts.
Work in St st worked in the rnd until Hat is approx 11"/28cm long.
Last Round: *K 2 sts together; rep from * around—you'll have
21 sts.
Thread yarn tail through rem sts and pull to gather, then knot
securely.

FINISHING
Weave in ends. •

Garter Pouf

Basic

MEASUREMENTS
Circumference Approx 19"/61cm
Height Approx 4"/48.5cm

MATERIALS
Yarn
LION BRAND® *Wool-Ease*®, *Thick & Quick*® 6oz/170g skeins, each 106yd/97m (acrylic, wool) **6**
• 1 skein in #099 Fisherman

Needles
• One pair size 13 (9mm) knitting needles, *or size to obtain gauge*

Notions
• Tapestry needle
• Fiberfill stuffing

GAUGE
9 sts + 12 rows = 4"/10cm in garter st (k all sts in every row) using size 13 (9mm) needles. *BE SURE TO CHECK YOUR GAUGE*

NOTE
The Pouf is made from a garter st rectangle. When you're done knitting, you sew the first row (along the cast-on edge) to the last row (the bound-off edge) to make a tube. Then just follow the instructions in the Finishing section to gather the ends of the tube and add stuffing.

POUF
Cast on 15 sts.
Work in garter st until piece measures approx 17"/43cm from beginning. Bind off. Cut yarn, leaving a long yarn tail.

FINISHING
Thread yarn tail into blunt needle, then sew cast-on edge to bound-off edge to form a tube. Fasten off, but do not cut tail. Weave yarn tail in and out through stitches along one edge of tube, draw stitches tightly together and knot to secure.
Stuff with fiberfill stuffing. Weave needle in and out through stitches around remaining open edge of tube and draw up tightly. Fasten off. Weave yarn ends to inside of Pouf. •

Beginner Scarf

Basic

MEASUREMENTS
Circumference Approx 7"/18cm × 65"/165cm

MATERIALS
Yarn
LION BRAND® *Homespun*®, *Thick & Quick*® 8oz/227g skeins, each 160yd/146cm (acrylic, polyester) **⑥**
• 1 skein in #436 Claret

Needles
• One pair size 13 (9mm) knitting needles, *or size to obtain gauge*

Notion
• Tapestry needle

GAUGE
• 8 stitches and 13 rows = 4"/10 cm in garter st (k all sts in every row) using size 13 (9mm) needles. *BE SURE TO CHECK YOUR GAUGE.*

SCARF
Cast on 14 stitches.
Work in Garter stitch until piece measures about 65"/165cm from beginning.
Bind off.

FINISHING
Weave in ends. •

Super-Quick Mitts

Basic

MEASUREMENTS
Circumference Approx 7½"/19cm
Length Approx 6½"/16.5cm

MATERIALS
Yarn
LION BRAND® *Wool-Ease®*, *Thick & Quick®* 6oz/170g skeins; each
106yd/97m (acrylic, wool)
• 1 skein in #143 Claret

Needles
• One set (5) double-pointed needles (dpn) size 13 (9mm), *or size to obtain gauge*

Notions
• Stitch markers
• Tapestry needle

GAUGE
9 sts = 4"/10cm, using size 13 (9mm) dpn. *BE SURE TO CHECK YOUR GAUGE.*

NOTE
Mitts are worked in the round on double-pointed needles (dpn).

MITTS (MAKE 2)
Cast on 16 sts and divide sts onto 4 needles with 4 sts on each needle. Place marker for beginning of rnd and join by working the first st on the left-hand needle with the working yarn from the right-hand needle and being careful not to twist sts.
Rnds 1–6 *K2, p2; rep from * around—16 sts.
Rnds 7–14 Knit.
Note Work will now proceed in rows to create a thumb hole.
Row 15 Knit to end of rnd, turn.
Row 16 Purl.
Rows 17 and 18 Repeat Rows 15 and 16. Resume working in rnds at the end of Row 18.
Rnds 19 and 20 Knit.
Rnds 21 and 22 Purl.
Bind off.

FINISHING
Weave in ends. •

Simple Ribbed Hat

Easy

SIZES
Child S (Child M/L, Adult S/M, Adult L). Pattern is written for smallest size with changes for larger sizes in parentheses.

MEASUREMENTS
Circumference Approx 16 (18, 20, 22)"/40.5 (45.5, 51, 56)cm, will stretch to fit a range of sizes.
Height Approx 7 (7½, 10 1/2, 10¾)"/18 (19, 26.5, 27.5)cm, height can be customized.

MATERIALS
Yarn
LION BRAND® *Wool-Ease®, Thick & Quick®* 6oz/170g skeins, each approx 106yd/97m (acrylic, wool) **(6)**
• 1 (1, 1, 1) skein in #402 Wheat

Needles
• One set (5) double-pointed needles (dpn) size 13 (9mm), *or size to obtain gauge*

Notions
• Stitch markers
• Tapestry needle

GAUGE
9 sts = 4"/10cm in St st worked in rnds (k every rnd), using size 13 (9mm) dpn. *BE SURE TO CHECK YOUR GAUGE.*

K1, P1 RIB WORKED IN THE ROUND
(even number of sts)
Rnd 1 *K1, p1; rep from * to end of rnd.
Rep Rnd 1 for K1, p1 Rib worked in rnds.

K2, P2 RIB WORKED IN THE ROUND
(multiple of 4 sts)
Rnd 1 *K2, p2; rep from * to end of rnd.
Rep Rnd 1 for K2, p2 Rib worked in rnds.

K3, P1 RIB WORKED IN THE ROUND
(multiple of 4 sts)
Rnd 1 (RS) *K3, p1; rep from * to end of rnd.
Rep Rnd 1 for K3, p1 Rib worked in rnds.

NOTES
1) This pattern is a recipe for making a custom hat. You choose your size and length and which rib pattern you'd like.
2) Hat is worked in rnds on double-pointed needles (dpn) beg at lower edge.

BASIC HAT
Cast on 36 (40, 44, 48) sts. Divide sts onto 4 needles, placing 9 (10, 11, 12) sts on each needle. Place marker for beg of rnd. Join by working the first st on left hand needle with the working yarn from the right hand needle and being careful not to twist sts.
Choose one of the Rib Patterns, and work until piece measures 1½ (1½, 2, 2)"/4 (4, 5, 5)cm from beg or desired length. For our sample, we chose to use K3, p1 Rib worked in rnds.
Change to St st worked in rnds until piece measures about 6¾ (7½, 10½, 10½)"/17 (18.5, 26, 26.5)cm from beg or desired length.

Shape Crown (Top of Hat)
Dec Rnd K2tog around—18 (20, 22, 24) sts at the end of this rnd.
Cut yarn, leaving a long yarn tail. Thread tail through remaining sts and pull to gather. Knot securely.

FINISHING
Weave in ends. •

Misty Haze Cowl

Basic

MEASUREMENTS
Circumference Approx 69"/175.5cm
Height Approx 18"/45.5cm

MATERIALS
Yarn
LION BRAND® *Shawl in a Ball*®, 5.3oz/150g skeins; each 481yd/440m (acrylic, cotton) (4)
• 1 skein in #302 Prism

Needles
• One pair size 10½ (6.5mm) knitting needles, *or size to obtain gauge*

Notion
• Tapestry needle

GAUGE
12 sts = 4"/10cm in St st (k on RS, p on WS), using size 10½ (6.5mm) needles. *BE SURE TO CHECK YOUR GAUGE.*

NOTES
1) Cowl is worked in one piece on large needles.
2) Ends of piece are sewn together to make the Cowl.

COWL
Cast on 54 sts.
Row 1 (RS) Slip the first st, knit to end of row.
Row 2 Slip the first st, work in St st to end of row.
Repeat Row 2 until about 2yd/2m of yarn remains.
Bind off.

FINISHING
Sew ends of piece together to make Cowl.
Weave in ends. •

Tassel-Trimmed Pillow

Basic

MEASUREMENTS
Approx 16"/40.5cm x 16"/40.5cm

MATERIALS
Yarn
LION BRAND® *Mandala*®, 5.3oz/150g skeins; each 590yd/540m (acrylic) (3)
• 1 skein in #209 Gnome

Needles
• One pair size 5 (3.75mm) knitting needles), *or size to obtain gauge*

Notions
• Tapestry needle
• 16"/40.5cm square pillow form
• 4"/10cm square piece of piece of cardboard

GAUGE
22 sts = 4"/10cm in Stockinette st (knit on RS, purl on WS), using size 5 (3.75mm) needles. *BE SURE TO CHECK YOUR GAUGE.*

NOTES
1) Front and Back of Pillow are worked separately.
2) A tassel is tied to each corner of Pillow.

PILLOW FRONT
Cast on 88 sts.
Work in St st until piece measures approx 16"/40.5cm from beg. Bind off.

PILLOW BACK
Cast on and work same as Front.

FINISHING
Tassels (make 4)
Wrap yarn around cardboard about 30 times.
Cut an 8"/20.5cm length of yarn and thread into blunt needle. Insert needle under all strands at upper edge of cardboard. Pull tightly and knot securely near strands.
Cut yarn loops at edge of cardboard. Cut another 8"/20.5cm length of yarn and wrap tightly around loops approx ¾"/2cm below top knot to form Tassel neck. Knot securely; thread ends into needle and weave ends to center of Tassel. Trim Tassel ends evenly.

Assembly
Sew Front and Back tog along 3 sides.
Thread yarn tails on each Tassel into needle, then sew a Tassel to each corner of Pillow.
Weave in ends.
Insert pillow form into open side of Pillow and sew closed. •

Neckwarmer with a Twist

Basic

MEASUREMENTS
Circumference Approx 37"/94cm
Height Approx 5½"/14cm

MATERIALS
Yarn
LION BRAND® *Wool-Ease®*, *Thick & Quick®* 6oz/170g skeins; each 106yd/97m (acrylic, wool) **6**
• 1 skein in #402 Wheat

Needle
• One size 11 (8mm) circular needle, 29"/73.5cm long, *or size to obtain gauge.*

Notions
• Stitch markers
• Tapestry needle

GAUGE
13 sts + 14 rnds = about 4"/10cm over pattern using size 11 (8mm) needle. *BE SURE TO CHECK YOUR GAUGE.*

NOTE
Neckwarmer is worked in one piece in the round.

NECKWARMER
Cast on 120 sts. Place marker for beginning of rnd. Turn one end over (180-degree turn) to put a twist in the cast-on. Keeping the twist, join by working the first stitch on the left-hand needle with the working yarn from the right hand.
Rnd 1 *Knit 2 sts, purl 2 sts; repeat from * around.
Repeat Rnd 1 until piece measures approx 5½"/14cm from beginning.
Bind off.

FINISHING
Weave in ends. •

Perfectly Simple Rectangle Shawl

Basic

MEASUREMENTS

Approx 19"/48.5cm x 46"/117cm

MATERIALS

Yarn

LION BRAND® *Shawl in a Ball*®, 5.3oz/150g skeins; each 481yd/440m (acrylic, cotton) 4

• 1 skein in #207 Feng Shui

Needles

• One pair size 10½ (6.5mm) knitting needles, *or size to obtain gauge*

Notion

• Tapestry needle

GAUGE

17 sts = 4"/10cm over St st (k on RS, p on WS), using size 10½ (6.5mm) needles. *BE SURE TO CHECK YOUR GAUGE.*

NOTE

Shawl is worked back and forth in one piece at a loose gauge to create an airy drape.

SHAWL

Loosely cast on 80 sts.
Work in St st until only about 30"/76cm of yarn remains.
Bind off loosely.

FINISHING

Blocking

Dampen Shawl thoroughly. Spread a towel onto a flat surface, then lay Shawl onto towel and smooth into shape. Gently shape Shawl to match finished measurements. Use blocking wires if desired to further shape Shawl. Allow to air dry.
Weave in ends. •

Phone Sweater

Basic

MEASUREMENTS

Approx 3½"/9cm x 5½"/14cm after folding and seaming

MATERIALS

Yarn

LION BRAND® *Vanna's Choice*®, 3½oz/100g skeins, each 170yd/156m (acrylic, rayon) (4)
• 1 skein #401 Grey Marble
Note One skein of yarn will make multiple Sweaters!

Needles

• One pair size 8 (5mm) knitting needles, *or size to obtain gauge*

Notions

• 2 toggle-style buttons
• Tapestry needle

GAUGE

16 sts = 4"/10cm over pattern, using size 8 (5mm) needles. *BE SURE TO CHECK YOUR GAUGE.*

SWEATER

Cast on 16 sts.
Knit 7 rows.
Next Row Purl.
Next Row Knit.
Rep last 2 rows until piece measures approx 7½"/19cm from beg, end with a knit row as the last row you work.
Next Row P5, k6, p5.
Next Row Knit.
Rep last 2 rows five more times.

Front neck, first half

Next Row (WS) P5, k3, slip the rem 8 sts to a scrap piece of yarn, these will make the second half of the neck.
Row 1 K the 8 sts still on your needle.
Row 2 P5, k3.
Rows 3 and 4 Rep Rows 1 and 2.
Row 5 K3, k the next 2 sts together, k3.
Row 6 P4, k3.
Row 7 K3, k2tog, k2.
Bind off.

Front neck, second half

Sl the 8 sts for the second half of the neck back onto your needle and join the yarn so that you are ready to work a WS row.
Next Row K3, p5.
Row 1 Knit.
Row 2 K3, p5.
Rows 3 and 4 Rep Rows 1 and 2.
Row 5 K3, k the next 2 sts tog, k3.
Row 6 K3, p4.
Row 7 K2, k the next 2 sts tog, k3.
Bind off.

FINISHING

Fold piece in half and sew sides.
Sew buttons to front of Sweater.

Weave in ends. •

Seed-Stitch Hat

Basic

MEASUREMENTS

Circumference Approx 19"/48.5cm
Height Approx 11"/28cm
Note Hat will stretch to fit a range of sizes.

MATERIALS

Yarn

LION BRAND® *Wool-Ease®*, *Thick & Quick®*, 5oz/140g skeins; each 87yd/80m (acrylic, wool) **6**
• 1 skein in #612 Coney Island

Needles

• One set (5) double-pointed needles (dpn) size 11 (8mm), *or size to obtain gauge*

Notions

• Tapestry needle
• Stitch holders

GAUGE

9 stitches = 4"/10cm over seed st in the rnd, using size 11 (8mm) dpn. *BE SURE TO CHECK YOUR GAUGE.*

SEED STITCH IN THE ROUND

Rnd 1 K1, *p1, k1; rep from * around.
Rnd 2 P1, *k1, p1; rep from * around.
Rep Rnds 1 and 2 for seed st in the rnd.

NOTES

1) Hat is worked in one piece in the round on double-pointed knitting needles. If you prefer, you can work the hat on a 16"/40.5cm long circular needle, then change to double-pointed needles to work the last round.
2) The edge of the Hat is worked in Stockinette stitch worked in the round (knit every stitch on every round) and will roll; the rest of the Hat is worked in seed stitch.

HAT

Cast 43 sts onto 4 of the dpn—with 10 sts on 1 needle and 11 sts on each of 3 needles.
Pm for the beg of the rnd. Join by working the first st on the left-hand needle with the working yarn from the right-hand needle and being careful not to twist the sts.

As you k the Hat, sl the marker as you come to it on each rnd. Work in St st worked in the rnd (k every st on every rnd) for 5 rnds. Work in seed st in the rnd until you have approx 1yd/1m) of yarn rem.
Last Rnd K1, *p2tog, k2 sts tog; rep from * around—22 sts. Thread yarn tail through rem sts and pull to gather, then knot securely.

FINISHING

Weave in ends. •

Bejeweled Beanie

Basic

MEASUREMENTS

Circumference Approx 19½"/49.5cm
Height Approx Approx 10"/25.5cm
Note Beanie will stretch to fit a range of sizes.

MATERIALS

Yarn

LION BRAND® *Wool-Ease® Thick & Quick®*, 6oz/170g skeins, each approx 92yd/84m (acrylic/wool) **6**
• 1 skein in #303 Constellation

Needles
• One set (5) double-pointed needles (dpn) size 13 (9mm), *or size to obtain gauge*

Notions
• Stitch markers
• Tapestry needle
• 4 sew-on rhinestone beads
• Sewing needle and thread

GAUGE

9 sts = 4"/10cm in St st worked in rnds (k every rnd), using size 13 (9mm) dpn. *BE SURE TO CHECK YOUR GAUGE.*

LAZY DAISY STITCH

Bring threaded blunt needle through from WS to RS of Beanie. This point is the base of the petal. *Insert needle as closely as possible to base of petal, then bring needle back up at tip of petal, looping yarn under needle. Pull needle away from you. Insert needle into Beanie just over the looped yarn. Take needle to the WS to anchor the stitch; repeat from * for each petal. Make as many petals as desired.

NOTES

1) Beanie is worked in one piece in the round on double-pointed needles.
2) Flowers are embroidered onto the Beanie, then a bead is sewn to the center of each flower.

BEANIE

With A, cast on 44 sts. Divide sts onto 4 needles, with 11 sts on each needle. Place marker for beginning of rnd. Join by working

the first st on the left hand needle with the working yarn from the right hand needle and being careful not to twist sts.
Work in St st worked in rnds (k every rnd) until piece measures about 11"/28cm from beginning.

Shape Crown (top of Beanie)
Decrease Rnd 1 Knit 2 sts together around—22 sts.
Decrease Rnd 2 Repeat Rnd 1.

Cut yarn, leaving a long yarn tail. Thread yarn tail through remaining 11 sts and pull to gather. Knot yarn.

FINISHING

Embroider 4 Lazy Daisy flowers onto Beanie. With sewing needle and thread, sew a bead to the center of each flower.
Weave in ends. •

Ribbed Cowl

Basic

MEASUREMENTS
Circumference Approx 66"/167.5cm
Height Approx 7"/18cm

MATERIALS
Yarn
LION BRAND® *Mandala*®, 5.3oz/150g skeins; each 590yd/540m (acrylic) ③
• 1 skein in #209 Gnome

Needles
• One pair size 7 (4.5mm) knitting needles, *or size to obtain gauge*

Notion
• Tapestry needle

GAUGE
32 sts = 4"/10cm over Rows 1 and 2 of pattern, using size 7 (4.5mm) needles. *BE SURE TO CHECK YOUR GAUGE.*

NOTES
Cowl is worked in one piece, then ends are sewn together to make a ring.

COWL
Cast on 57 sts.
Row 1 K3, *p3, k3; rep from * to end of row.
Row 2 P3, *k3, p3; rep from * to end of row.

Rep Rows 1 and 2 until about 3yd/3m of yarn rem.
Bind off all sts and pull yarn tail through rem sts.

Thread yarn tail into blunt needle, then sew ends of Cowl tog to make a ring.

FINISHING
Weave in ends. •

Seed-Rib Hat

●●

Easy

MEASUREMENTS
Circumference Approx 17"/43cm, along lower ribbed edge and unstretched
Height Approx 9½"/24cm
Note Hat will stretch to fit a range of sizes.

MATERIALS
Yarn
LION BRAND® *Touch of Merino*®, 3½ oz/100g skeins; each 257yd/235m (acrylic, merino wool)
• 1 skein in #150 Oxford Grey

Needles
• One size 4 (3.5mm) circular needle, 16"/40.5cm long, *or size to obtain gauge*
• One set (5) double-pointed needles (dpn) size 4 (3.5mm), *or size to obtain gauge*

Notions
• Stitch markers
• Tapestry needle

GAUGE
28 sts = 4"/10cm over Rib Rnd 1, using size 4 (3.5mm) needle.
BE SURE TO CHECK YOUR GAUGE.

SEED RIB
Rnd 1 *K2, p1, k1, p1; repeat from * around.
Rnd 2 *K2, k1, p1, k1; repeat from * around.

NOTES
1) Hat is worked in one piece, from lower edge to top of Hat, beginning on a circular needle then changing to double-pointed needles when sts have been sufficiently decreased.
2) The lower edge of the Hat is worked in k1, p1 rib, then the body of the Hat is worked in a Seed Rib.
3) The Hat is very stretchy and will fit most sizes.

HAT
With circular needle, cast on 120 sts.
Place a marker for beginning of round. Join by working the first stitch on the left hand needle with the working yarn from the right hand needle and being careful not to twist stitches.
When knitting the Hat, always slip the marker as you come to it.

Ribbed edge
Rib Rnd 1 *Knit 1, purl 1; repeat from * around.
Repeat Rnd 1 for about 1½"/4cm.

Seed Rib
Work in seed rib until piece measures approx 9"/23cm from beg; end with a Rnd 1 of Seed Rib as the last rnd you work.

Shape Top of Hat
Next Rnd *K2, p3tog; rep from * around—72 sts.
Next Rnd *K2, p1; rep from * around.
Note As you work the next rnd, you'll need to change from the circular needle to the dpn. Do this by simply using one dpn at a time to work the sts off the circular needle. Don't forget to move your st marker onto the dpn as well!
Next Rnd *K2tog, p1; rep from * around—48 sts.
Next Rnd *K1, p1; rep from * around
Next Rnd K2tog around—24 sts.
Cut yarn, leaving a long yarn tail. Thread tail into blunt needle. Draw needle through rem sts as you remove the sts from the needles.
Pull yarn tail to close opening at top of Hat and knot.

FINISHING
Weave in ends. •

Movie Night Circle Scarfie

Easy

MEASUREMENTS
Circumference Approx 14"/35.5cm, unstretched
Height Approx 9"/23cm

MATERIALS
Yarn
LION BRAND® *Landscapes*®, 3½oz/100g skeins; each 147yd/134m
(acrylic) **4**
• 1 skein in #200 Tropics

Needles
• One set (5) double-pointed needles (dpn) size 10 (6mm), *or size to obtain gauge*

Notions
• Stitch markers
• Tapestry needle

GAUGE
24 sts = 4"/10cm over Rnd 1 using size 10 (6mm) dpn. *BE SURE TO CHECK YOUR GAUGE.*

NOTE
Circle Scarfie is worked in one piece in the round on double-pointed knitting needles.

CIRCLE SCARFIE
Cast on 84 sts.
Divide sts onto 4 dpn, with 21 sts on each needle. Place marker for beginning of rnd and join by working the first st on the left-hand needle with the working yarn from the right-hand needle, and being careful not to twist sts.
Rnd 1 *K2, p2; rep from * around.
Rep Rnd 1 until piece measures approx 9"/23cm from beg.
Bind off.

FINISHING
Weave in ends. •

Ombré Scarfie

Basic

MEASUREMENTS
Approx 7"18cm x 68"/173cm

MATERIALS
Yarn

LION BRAND® *Scarfie*®, 5.3oz/150g skeins; each 312yd/285m (acrylic, wool) **5**
• 1 skein in #205 Cranberry/Black

Needles
• One pair size 9 (5.5mm) knitting needles, *or size to obtain gauge*

Notion
• Tapestry needle

GAUGE
19 stitches + 21 rows = 4"/10cm in pattern using size 9 (5.5mm) needles. *BE SURE TO CHECK YOUR GAUGE.*

SCARFIE
Cast on 33 sts.
Row 1 (K3, p3) to last 3 sts, knit last 3 sts.
Row 2 K the k stitches and p the p sts as they face you.
Rep Row 2 until about 1yd/1m of yarn rem.
Bind off.

FINISHING
Weave in ends. •

Pike Street Hat

●●
Easy

MEASUREMENTS
Circumference Approx 18"/45.5cm at ribbed edge
Height Approx 11½"/29cm
Note Hat will stretch to fit a range of sizes.

MATERIALS
Yarn
LION BRAND® *Wool-Ease*®, *Thick & Quick*®, 6oz/170g skeins; each 106yd/97m (acrylic, wool)
• 1 skein in #535 River Run

Needles
• One set (5) double-pointed needles (dpn) size 11 (8mm), *or size to obtain gauge*

Notions
• Stitch markers
• Tapestry needle

GAUGE
10 sts = 4"/10cm over St st worked in the rnd (knit every rnd), using size 11 (8mm) dpn. *BE SURE TO CHECK YOUR GAUGE.*

NOTE
Designer worked the Hat on double pointed needles—if you prefer, you can cast on with a size 11 (8mm) circular needle, 16"/40.5cm long, then switch to double-pointed needles to work the Shape Crown section.

HAT
Cast on 48 sts.
Divide sts onto 4 needles, with 12 sts on each needle.
Pm for beg of rnd.
Join by knitting the first st on the left-hand needle with the working yarn from the right-hand needle and being careful not to twist sts.
Sm at the end of each rnd.
Rnd 1: *K2, p2, rep from * around.
Rep Rnd 1 until piece measures approx 5½"/14cm from beg.
Change to St st worked in the rnd (k every rnd) and work until piece measures about 9"/23cm from beg.

Shape Crown (top of Hat)
Next Rnd *K6, k2tog, rep from * around—42 sts.
Knit 1 rnd.
Next Rnd *K5, k2tog, rep from * around—36 sts.
Knit 1 rnd.
Next Rnd *K4, k2tog, rep from * around—30 sts.
Knit 1 rnd.
Next Rnd *K3, k2tog, rep from * around—24 sts.
Knit 1 rnd.
Next Rnd *K2, k2tog, rep from * around—18 sts.
Knit 1 rnd.
Next Rnd K2tog around—9 sts.
Cut yarn, leaving a long yarn tail.
Thread tail into blunt needle and then through rem sts.
Pull to close top of Hat and knot.

FINISHING
Weave in ends. •

Eyelet Triangle Shawl

Easy

MEASUREMENTS
Approx 27"/68.5cm x 64"/162.5cm at longest and widest

MATERIALS

Yarn

LION BRAND® *Mandala*®, 5.3oz/150g skeins; each 590yd/540m (acrylic) **(3)**
• 1 skein in #217 Genie

Needle
• One size 8 (5mm) circular needle, 36"/91.5cm long, *or size to obtain gauge*

Notions
• Stitch markers
• Tapestry needle

GAUGE
18 sts = 4"/10cm over Rows 1–6 of pattern, using size 6 (4mm) needles. *BE SURE TO CHECK YOUR GAUGE.*

NOTES
1) Shawl is worked in one piece beginning at the neck edge.
2) A circular needle is used to accommodate the large number of stitches. Work back and forth on the circular needle as if working on straight needles.
3) Four yarn over increases are worked on every right-side row of Shawl.

SHAWL
Cast on 5 sts.
Knit 2 rows.
Set-Up Row (RS) K2, yo, place marker, k1, place marker, yo, k2—7 sts.
Next Row Slipping markers as you come to them, k2, purl to last 2 sts, k2.
Row 1 (Increase Row, RS) K2, yo, k to marker, yo, slip marker, k1, slip marker, yo, k to last 2 sts, yo, k2.
Rows 2 and 4 Slipping markers as you come to them, k2, purl to last 2 sts, k2.
Rows 3 and 5 Rep Row 1.

Row 6 (WS) Slipping markers as you come to them, knit across.
Repeat Rows 1–6 until piece along center st between markers measures approx 25½"/65cm, end with a Row 6 as the last row you work.

Border
Next Row K2, yo, k to marker, yo, slip marker, k1, slip marker, yo, k to last 2 sts, yo, k2.
Next Row (WS) Slipping markers as you come to them, knit across.
Repeat last 2 rows 3 more times—total of 8 rows worked for border. Bind off loosely.

FINISHING
Weave in ends. •

Quick Seed-Stitch Cowl

Easy

MEASUREMENTS
Circumference Approx 27"/68.5cm
Height Approx 10½"/26.5cm

MATERIALS
Yarn
LION BRAND® *Wool-Ease®*, *Thick & Quick®*, 6oz/170g skeins; each 106yd/97m (acrylic, wool) (6)
• 1 skein in #138 Cranberry

Needle
• One size 13 (9mm) circular needle, 16"/40.5cm long, *or size to obtain gauge*

Notions
• Stitch markers
• Tapestry needle

GAUGE
8 sts + 15 rnds = 4"/10cm over Rnds 1 and 2 using size 13 (9mm) needle. *BE SURE TO CHECK YOUR GAUGE.*

NOTES
1) Cowl is worked in the round on a circular knitting needle.
2) Edges of Cowl will roll gently to create an interesting edge.

COWL
Loosely cast on 53 sts. Place marker for beg of rnd and join by working first st on left-hand needle with working yarn from right-hand needle and being careful not to twist sts.
Knit 5 rnds.
Rnd 1 K1, *p1, k1; rep from * around.
Rnd 2 P1, *k1, p1; rep from * around.
Rep Rnds 1 and 2 for 12 more times.
Knit 5 rnds.
Bind off loosely.

FINISHING
Weave in ends. •

26

Seed-Stitch Slippers

Easy

SIZES
Women's S (M, L)
Approx women's shoe size 5–6 (7–8, 9–10). Pattern is written for smallest size with changes for larger sizes in parentheses.

MEASUREMENTS
Length Approx 9 (10, 11)"/23 (25.5, 28)cm
Note Length is adjustable.

MATERIALS
Yarn
LION BRAND® *Wool-Ease®*, *Thick & Quick®*, 6oz/170g skeins; each 106yd/97m (acrylic, wool) 6
• 1 skein in #402 Wheat

Needles
• One pair size 11 (8mm) knitting needles, *or size to obtain gauge*

Notion
• Tapestry needle
• Two large buttons

GAUGE
9 sts = 4"/10cm in St st (K on RS, p on WS), using size 11 (8mm) needles. *BE SURE TO CHECK YOUR GAUGE.*

STITCH GLOSSARY
Seed Stitch
(odd number of sts)
Row 1 *K1, p1; repeat from * to last st, k1.
Row 2 K the purl sts and p the knit sts.
Repeat Row 2 for Seed st.

NOTES
1) Slippers are worked flat and then seamed. Diagrams for seaming are provided.
2) Soles of Slippers are worked in Stockinette stitch and sides are worked in Seed stitch.
3) Slipper soles are shaped with easy increases—you just knit into the front and then the back of a single stitch—thus making 1 stitch into 2 stitches.
4) Slipper toes are shaped with 2 different decreases.

SLIPPERS (MAKE 2)
Cast on 17 sts.
Knit one row for back seam of Slipper.

Next Row (WS) Work in seed st over first 5 sts, p to last 5 sts, work in Seed st over last 5 sts.

Next (Increase) Row Work in seed st over first 5 sts, k into front of next st but do not remove it from the left hand needle, knit into back of same st (increase made); k to last 6 sts, increase in next st (just as before, knitting into both the front and the back of the stitch), work in seed st over last 5 sts. At the end of this row you'll have a total of 19 sts on your needle.

Seed-Stitch Slippers

Keeping the first and last 5 sts in seed st and the center 9 sts in St st, work until piece measures about 3"/7.5cm from beginning, end with a WS row as the last row you work.

Next Row (RS) Repeat the increase row—you'll now have 21 sts on your needle.

Continue working, keeping the first and last 5 sts in seed st and the center 11 sts in St st until piece measures about 8½ (9½, 10½)"/21.5 (24, 26.5)cm from beginning (or just a little less than the length of your foot), end with a WS row as the last row you work.

Shape Toe
Next Row (RS) Work in seed st over first 4 sts, k2tog, ssk, k5 sts, ssk, k2tog, work in seed st over last 4 sts.
At the end of this row you'll be left with 17 sts on your needle.
Bind off.
Cut yarn, leaving a long yarn tail.

FINISHING
Fold Slipper in half lengthwise.

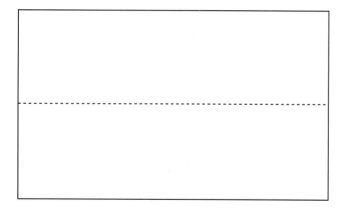

From the RS, sew the sides of the cast-on edge together with running stitch to make the heel. The seam on the RS is part of the design of the Slipper.
Beginning at the toe end of the Slipper, sew the sides together for 2½"/6.5cm to make the top of the foot.

Flatten Slipper so that the seam at the top of the foot is centered. Seam toe end of Slipper. Sew on buttons.

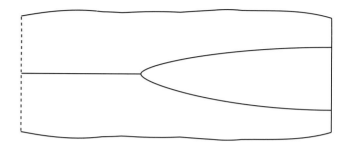

Weave in ends. •

Classic Ribbed Hat

●●
Easy

MEASUREMENTS
Circumference Approx 18½"/47cm
Height Approx 9"/23cm
Note Hat will stretch to fit a range of sizes.

MATERIALS
Yarn
LION BRAND® Wool-Ease®, Thick & Quick® 6oz/170g skeins; each 106yd/97m (acrylic, wool)
• 1 skein in #402 Wheat

Needles
• One size 11 (8mm) circular needle, 16"/40cm long, *or size to obtain gauge.*
• One set (5) double-pointed needles (dpn) size 11 (8mm), *or size to obtain gauge.*

Notions
• Stitch markers
• Tapestry needle

GAUGE
13 sts + 14 rnds = 4"/10cm over K2, p2 rib, slightly stretched, using size 11 (8mm) needle. *BE SURE TO CHECK YOUR GAUGE.*

STITCH GLOSSARY
Skp Slip 1 as if to knit, knit 1, pass slip stitch over knit stitch—1 st decreased.
Sk2p (slip-k2tog-pass slipped st over) A double decrease worked as follows:
1. Insert right needle as if to knit, and slip the next st from the left needle to the right needle.
2. Knit the next 2 sts together.
3. With tip of left needle, lift the slipped st (the 2nd st on right needle) up and over the k2tog (first st on right needle) and off the needle—you have decreased 2 sts.

NOTE
Hat is worked in one piece in the round, first on circular needle, then changing to double-pointed needles (dpn).

HAT
With circular needle, cast on 55 sts. Pm for beg of rnd and join by working the first st on the left-hand needle with the working yarn from the right-hand needle, being careful not to twist.
Rnd 1 *K2, p1, k2, p2, k2, p2; rep from * around.
Rnd 2 Rep Rnd 1.
Rnd 3 (Inc) *K2, M1P, p1, (k2, p2) twice; rep from * around—60 sts at the end of this rnd.
Rnds 4-9 Work in K2, p2 Rib.
Rnd 10 (Inc) *K2, M1P, p2, (k2, p2) twice; rep from * around—65 sts.
Rnd 11 *K2, p3, (k2, p2) twice; rep from * around.
Rep Rnd 11 until piece measures about 6"/15cm from beg.

Shape Crown (top of Hat)
Rnd 1 (Dec) *K1, skp, p1, k2tog, k1, work in rib as established over next 6 sts; rep from * around—55 sts.
Rnd 2 K the knit sts and p the purl sts.
Rnd 3 (Dec) *K1, sk2p, work in rib as established over next 7 sts; rep from * around—45 sts.
Change to dpn as you work the next rnd, with 15 sts on each of 3 needles.
Rnd 4 Rep Rnd 2.
Rnd 5 (Dec) *Sk2p, work in rib as established over next 6 sts; rep from * around—35 sts.
Rnd 6 Rep Rnd 2.
Rnd 7 (Dec) *P2tog, work in rib as established over next 5 sts; rep from * around—30 sts.
Rnd 8 (Dec) *P2tog, work in rib as established over next 4 sts; rep from * around—25 sts.
Rnd 9 (Dec) *P1, k2, p2tog; rep from * around—20 sts.
Rnd 10 (Dec) *K2tog, skp; rep from * around—10 sts.
Rnd 11 (Dec) *K2tog; rep from * around—5 sts.
Cut yarn, leaving a long yarn tail. Thread yarn tail through remaining sts and pull tight to gather. Knot securely.

FINISHING
Weave in ends. •

Pennant Scarf

Easy

MEASUREMENTS
Approx 19"/48.5cm x 60"/152.5cm at widest and longest

MATERIALS
Yarn

LION BRAND® *Mandala*®, 5.3oz/150g skeins; each 590yd/540m (acrylic) (3)
• 1 skein in #213 Wizard

Needles
• One pair size 6 (4mm) knitting needles, *or size to obtain gauge*

Notion
• Tapestry needle

GAUGE
18 sts = 4"/10cm over Rows 1–6 of pattern, using size 6 (4mm) needles. *BE SURE TO CHECK YOUR GAUGE.*

NOTES
1) Scarf is worked in one piece with yarn over increases along one edge for shaping.
2) The Scarf is worked in garter stitch (knit every stitch on every row), so is reversible.

SCARF
Cast on 5 sts.
Rows 1–4 Knit.
Row 5 K2, yo, knit to end of row—6 sts.
Row 6 Knit to last 3 sts, knit the yarn over through the back loop, knit 2.
Repeat Rows 1–6 until about 2yd/2m of yarn remains.
Bind off loosely.

FINISHING
Weave in ends. •

Cabled Mug Cozy

Easy

MEASUREMENTS

Approx 3½"/9cm x 9½"/24cm, to fit a standard coffee or tea mug

MATERIALS

Yarn

LION BRAND® *Vanna's Choice*®, 3½ oz/100g skeins; each 170yd/156m (acrylic, rayon) (4)
• 1 skein in #113 Scarlet

Note Yarn amount is sufficient to make 4-5 Cozies.

Needles

• One pair size 9 (5.5mm) knitting needles, *or size to obtain gauge*

Notions

• Cable needle
• Tapestry needle
• One small button
• Sewing needle and thread

GAUGE

18 sts + 28 rows = 4"/10cm in cable pattern using size 9 (5.5mm) needles. *BE SURE TO CHECK YOUR GAUGE.*

STITCH GLOSSARY

2/2 LC (2 over 2 left cross) Slip 2 sts to cable needle and hold in front, k2, then k2 from cable needle.

COZY

Cast on 52 sts.

Row 1 (WS) *P2, k2, p4, k2; rep from * to last 2 sts, p2.

Row 2 *K2, p2, k4, p2; rep from * to last 2 sts, k2.

Row 3 Rep Row 1.

Row 4 *K2, p2, 2/2 LC, p2; rep from * to last 2 sts, k2.

Rep Rows 1–4 until piece measures about 1¾"/4.5cm from beg, end with a Row 1 or 3 as the last row you work.

Next (Buttonhole) Row K2tog, yo, work in pattern as established to end of row.

Continue to work in pattern as established until piece measures approx 3½"/9cm from beg.

Bind off.

FINISHING

Sew sides of Cozy together for about ½"/1.5cm at top and at bottom, leaving remaining 2½"/6.5cm open for mug handle. With sewing needle and thread, sew button onto edge of handle opening, opposite buttonhole. •

Year of the Dog Sweater

Intermediate

SIZES

Size S (M, L, XL). Pattern is written for smallest size with changes for larger sizes in parentheses.

MEASUREMENTS

Neck Circumference Approx 11½ (14 1/2, 18, 20½)"/29 (37, 45.5, 52)cm

Chest Circumference Approx 16½ (19, 23, 28)"/42 (48.5, 58.5, 71)cm

Length Approx 12½ (14, 17 1/2, 20)"/32 (35.5, 44.5, 51)cm, not including hood

MATERIALS

Yarn

LION BRAND® *Homespun*®, 6oz/170g skeins; each 185yd/169m (acrylic, polyester) (5)

• 1 (2, 2, 3) skein in #309 Deco

Needles

• One pair size 10 (6mm) knitting needles, *or size to obtain gauge*
• One set (5) double-pointed needles (dpn) size 10 (6mm), *or size to obtain gauge*

Notion

• Stitch markers
• Tapestry needle

GAUGE

13 sts + 19 rows = 4"/10cm in bobble pattern, using size 10 (6mm) needles. *BE SURE TO CHECK YOUR GAUGE.*

STITCH GLOSSARY

MB (Make Bobble) (K1, k1 tbl, k1) all in the next st, turn; (sl 1, k2, turn) 3 times; sk2p.

sk2p (slip-k2tog-pass slipped st over) A double decrease worked as follows:

1. Insert right needle as if to knit, and sl the next st from the left needle to the right needle.

2. K the next 2 sts tog.

3. With tip of left needle, lift the slipped st (the 2nd st on right needle) up and over the k2tog (first st on right needle) and off the needle—2 sts decreased.

BACK

With straight needles, cast on 33 (37, 45, 53) sts.

Begin Bobble Pattern

Row 1 (WS) Knit.

Row 2 K2, MB, *k3, MB; rep from * to last 2 sts, k2—you will have 8 (9, 11, 13) bobbles at the end of this row.

Row 3 K2, p1 tbl, *k3, p1 tbl; rep from * to last 2 sts, k2.

Rows 4 and 5 Knit.

Row 6 K4, *MB, k3; rep from * to last st, k1—7 (8, 10, 12) bobbles.

Row 7 K4, *p1 tbl, k3; rep from * to last st, k1.

Row 8 Knit.

Rows 9-40 (48, 64, 72) Rep Rows 1–8 for Bobble pattern 4 (5, 7, 8) more times.

Place a marker on each end of last row worked.

Shape Top

Row 1 Knit.

Row 2 (Decrease Row—RS) K2tog, *MB, k3; rep from * to last 3 sts, MB, k2tog—8 (9, 11, 13) bobbles.

Row 3 K1, p1 tbl, *k3, p1 tbl; rep from * to last st, k1.

Row 4 (Decrease Row—RS) K1, k2tog, k to last 3 sts, k2tog, k1—29 (33, 41, 49) sts.

Row 5 Knit.

Row 6 K2, MB, *k3, MB; rep from * to last 2 sts, k2—7 (8, 10, 12) bobbles.

Row 7 K2, p1 tbl, *k3, p1 tbl; rep from * to last 2 sts, k2.

Row 8 (Decrease Row—RS) K1, k2tog, k to last 3 sts, k2tog, k1—27 (31, 39, 47) sts.

Row 9 Knit.

Row 10 (Decrease Row—RS) K1, k2tog, *MB, k3; rep from * to last 4 sts, MB, k2tog, k1—6 (7, 9, 11) bobbles.

SIZE XL ONLY

Rep Rows 7–10—10 bobbles.

ALL SIZES

Next Row K2, *p1 tbl, k3; rep from * to last 3 sts, p1 tbl, k2.

Next 2 Rows Knit.

Next Row (Decrease Row—RS) K1, k2tog, k1, *MB, k3; rep from * to last 5 sts, MB, k1, k2tog, k1—5 (6, 8, 9) bobbles.

Next Row K3, *p1 tbl, k3; rep from * to last 4 sts, p1 tbl, k3.
Next 2 Rows Knit.
Next Row K1, MB, *k3, MB; rep from * to last st, k1—6 (7, 9, 10) bobbles.
Next Row K1, p1 tbl, *k3, p1 tbl; rep from * to last st, k1.
Next Row (Increase Row—RS) K1, M1, k to last st, M1, k1—25 (29, 37, 41) sts.
Next Row Knit.
Next Row (Increase Row—RS) K1, MB, M1, k2, *MB, k3; rep from *

to last 5 sts, MB, k2, M1, MB, k1—7 (8, 10, 11) bobbles.
Next Row K1, *p1 tbl, k3; rep from * to last 2 sts, p1 tbl, k1.
Next Row (Increase Row—RS) K1, M1, k to last st, M1, k1—29 (33, 41, 45) sts.
Place a marker on each end of last row worked.

Shape Hood
Row 1 Knit.
Row 2 K4, *MB, k3; rep from * to last st, k1—6 (7, 9, 10) bobbles.

Year of the Dog Sweater

Row 3 K4, *p1 tbl, k3; rep from * to last st, k1.

Rows 4 and 5 Knit.

Row 6 K2, *MB, k3; rep from * to last 3 sts, MB, k2—7 (8, 10, 11) bobbles.

Row 7 K2, *p1 tbl, k3; rep from * to last 3 sts, p1 tbl, k2.

Row 8 Knit.

Row 9-16 (24, 32, 40) Rep Rows 1–8 for 1 (2, 3, 4) more times.

Shape Earholes

Row 1 Knit.

Row 2 (RS) K1, (k3, MB) 1 (1, 2, 2) time(s), k2, bind off next 4 sts, k1, MB, (k3, MB) 1 (2, 2, 3) times, k1, bind off next 4 sts, k2, (MB, k3) 1 (1, 2, 2) time(s), k1—4 (5, 7, 8) bobbles.

Row 3 K1, (k3, p1 tbl) 1 (1, 2, 2) time(s), k2, cast on 4 sts, k1, p1 tbl, (k3, p1 tbl) 1 (2, 2, 3) time(s), k1, cast on 4 sts, k2, (p1 tbl, k3) 1 (1, 2, 2) time(s), k1.

Rows 4 and 5 Knit.

Row 6 K2, *MB, k3; rep from * to last 3 sts, MB, k2—7 (8, 10, 11) bobbles.

Row 7 K2, *p1 tbl, k3; rep from * to last 3 sts, p1 tbl, k2.

Row 8 K1, *k2tog; rep from * across—15 (17, 21, 23) sts.

Bind off.

UNDERPIECE

With straight needles cast on 21 (25, 29, 37) sts.

Begin Bobble Pattern

Row 1 (WS) Knit.

Row 2 K2, MB, *k3, MB; rep from * to last 2 sts, k2—you will have 5 (6, 7, 9) bobbles at the end of this row.

Row 3 K2, p1 tbl, *k3, p1 tbl; rep from * to last 2 sts, k2.

Rows 4 and 5 Knit.

Row 6 K4, *MB, k3; rep from * to last st, k1—4 (5, 6, 8) bobbles.

Row 7 K4, *p1 tbl, k3; rep from * to last st, k1.

Row 8 Knit.

Rows 9–16 (24, 32, 40) Rep Rows 1–8 for Bobble pattern 1 (2, 3, 4) more times.

Next 3 Rows Rep Rows 1–3.

Place a marker on each end of last row worked.

Shape Top

Row 1 (Decrease Row—RS) K1, k2tog, k to last 3 sts, k2tog, k1—19 (23, 27, 35) sts.

Row 2 Knit.

Row 3 (Decrease Row) K1, k2tog, *MB, k3; rep from * to last 4 sts, MB, k2tog, k1—4 (5, 6, 8) bobbles.

Row 4 K2, *p1 tbl, k3; rep from * to last 3 sts, p1 tbl, k2.

SIZE XL ONLY

Rep Rows 1–4—7 bobbles.

ALL SIZES

Next Row (Decrease Row) K1, k2tog, k to last 3 sts, k2tog, k1—15 (19, 23, 27) sts.

Next Row Knit.

Next Row K3, *MB, k3; rep from * to end of row—3 (4, 5, 6) bobbles.

Next Row K3, *p1 tbl, k3; rep from * to end of row.

Next 2 Rows Knit.

Next Row K1, *MB, k3; rep from * to last 2 sts, MB, k1—4 (5, 6, 7) bobbles.

Next Row K1, *p1 tbl, k3; rep from * to last 2 sts, p1 tbl, k1.

Next Row (Increase Row—RS) K1, M1, k to last st, M1, k1—17 (21, 25, 29) sts.

Next Row Knit.

Next Row K4, *MB, k3; rep from * to last st, k1—3 (4, 5, 6) bobbles. Place a marker at each end of last row worked.

Next Row K4, *p1 tbl, k3; rep from * to last st, k1.

Next Row (Increase Row) K1, M1, k to last st, M1, k1—19 (23, 27, 31) sts.

Next Row Knit.

Next Row (Increase Row) K1, M1, k2, *MB, k3; rep from * to last 4 sts, MB, k2, M1, k1—4 (5, 6, 7) bobbles.

Bind off.

FINISHING

Sew Underpiece to Back at sides, leaving sides open between markers for leg openings. Leave remaining portions of Back unsewn for hood and lower back.

Leg Edging

Rnd 1 (RS) From RS with double pointed needles, pick up and k20 (20, 20, 24) sts evenly spaced around one leg opening. Divide sts onto 4 needles with 5 (5, 5, 6) sts on each needle. Place marker for beg of rnd and join by working the first st on the left hand needle with the working yarn from the right hand needle.

Rnd 2 Purl.

Rnd 3 Knit.

Rnds 4 and 5 Rep Rnds 2 and 3.

Rnd 6 Purl.

Rnd 7 (Decrease Rnd) (K2tog, k3) 4 times, (k2tog, k2) 0 (0, 0, 1) time—16 (16, 16, 19) sts.

Rnd 8 Purl.

Bind off.

Rep edging around other leg opening.

Weave in ends. •

Breath of Glitter Shawl

Easy

MEASUREMENTS
Approx 17"/43cm x 54"/137cm

MATERIALS
Yarn
LION BRAND® *Shawl in a Ball*®, 5.3oz/150g skeins; each 481yd/440m (acrylic, cotton) **4**
• 1 skein #303 Namaste Neutrals

Needles
• One pair size 10½ (6.5mm) knitting needles, *or size to obtain gauge*

Notions
• Tapestry needle

GAUGE
15 sts = 4"/10cm in pattern, using size 10½ (6.5mm) needles. *BE SURE TO CHECK YOUR GAUGE.*

STITCH GLOSSARY
Sk2p (slip-k2tog-pass slipped st over) A double decrease worked as follows:
1. Insert right needle as if to knit, and slip the next st from the left-hand needle to the right hand needle.
2. Knit the next 2 sts together.
3. With tip of left-hand needle, lift the slipped st (the 2nd st on right needle) up and over the k2tog (first st on right needle) and off the needle—you have decreased 2 sts.

NOTE
Shawl is worked in one piece in a very easy lace pattern.

SHAWL
Cast on 65 sts.
Row 1 (WS) K2, purl to last 2 sts, k2.
Row 2 (RS) K3, *yo, k1, sk2p, k1, yo, k1; rep from* to last 2 sts, k2.
Rep Rows 1 and 2 until about 2yd/2m of yarn rem.
Bind off.

FINISHING
Weave in ends. •

Cabled Heart Boot Cuffs

Easy

MEASUREMENTS
Circumference Approx 10"/25.5cm
Length Approx 6"/15cm
Note Cuffs will stretch to fit a range of sizes.

MATERIALS
LION BRAND® *Vanna's Choice*®, 3½oz/100g skeins, each 170yd/156m (acrylic, rayon) (4)
• 1 skein in #101 Pink

Needles
• One pair size 9 (5.5mm) knitting needles, *or size to obtain gauge*
• One pair size 10 (6mm) knitting needles, *or size to obtain gauge*

Notions
• Cable needle
• Tapestry needle

GAUGE
16 sts + 22 rows = 4"/10cm in St st (k on RS, p on WS) using size 9 (5.5) needles. *BE SURE TO CHECK YOUR GAUGE.*

STITCH GLOSSARY
2/1 LPC (2 over 1 left purl cross) Sl 2 sts to cable needle and hold in front of work, p1, then k2 from cable needle.
2/1 RPC (2 over 1 right purl cross) Sl 1 st to cable needle and hold in back of work, k2, then p1 from cable needle.
2/2 LC (2 over 2 left cross) Sl 2 sts to cable needle and hold in front of work, k2, then k2 from cable needle.
2/2 RC (2 over 2 right cross) Sl 2 sts to cable needle and hold in back of work, k2, then k2 from cable needle.
2/2 LPC (2 over 2 left cross) Sl 2 sts to cable needle and hold in front of work, p2, then k2 from cable needle.
2/2 RPC (2 over 2 right cross) Sl 2 sts to cable needle and hold in back of work, k2, then p2 from cable needle.

NOTE
Cuffs are worked flat then sides are seamed.

CUFFS (MAKE 2)
With smaller needles, cast on 56 sts.
Row 1 K1, *k2, p2, rep from * across.
Row 2 K the knit sts and p the purl sts to last st.
Rows 3–11 Rep Row 2.

Begin Heart Cables
Change to larger needles.
Row 12 (RS) K1, p4, *2/2RC, 2/2LC, p10; rep from * once more; 2/2RC, 2/2LC, p6, k1.
Rows 13, 15, 17, 19, 21 and 23 Rep Row 2.
Row 14 K1, p2, *2/2RPC, k4, 2/2LPC, p6; rep from * once more; 2/2RPC, k4, 2/2LPC, p4, k1.
Row 16 K1, p1, *2/1RPC, p2, 2/2RC, p2, 2/1LPC, p4; rep from * once more; 2/1RPC, p2, 2/2 RC, p2, 2/1LPC, p3, k1.
Row 18 K1, *2/1RPC, p3, k4, p3, 2/1LPC, p2; rep from * to last st, k1.
Row 20 K1, *k2, p4, 2/2RC, p4, k2, p2; rep from * to last st, k1.
Row 22 K1, *2/2LPC, 2/2RC, 2/2LC, 2/2RPC, p2; rep from * to last st, k1.
Row 24 *P2, k2; rep from * across.
Rows 25-31 Rep Row 2.
Bind off.

FINISHING
Sew sides of piece to make Cuff.
Weave in ends. •

Easy Half-Circle Shawl

Easy

MEASUREMENTS

Approx 22"/56cm x 46"/117cm, at widest and longest points

MATERIALS

Yarn

LION BRAND® *Shawl in a Ball*®, 5.3oz/150g skeins; each 481yd/440m (acrylic, cotton) 4
• 1 skein in #204 Healing Teal

Needle

• One size 8 (5mm) circular needle, 29"/73.5cm long, *or size to obtain gauge.*

Notions

• Stitch markers
• Tapestry needle

GAUGE

14 sts = 4"/10cm in St st (k on RS, p on WS), using size 8 (5mm) needle. *BE SURE TO CHECK YOUR GAUGE.*

NOTES

1) Half Circle Shawl is worked in one piece beginning at center back neck, and is shaped by working yarn over (yo) increases.
2) Shawl begins with a small rectangle of garter stitch (knit every row).
3) A circular needle is used to accommodate the large number of sts. Work back and forth in rows on the circular needle just as if working on straight needles.

SHAWL

Cast on 3 sts.

Working back and forth in rows on circular needle, work in garter st (knit every row) for 9 rows.

At the end of the last row, do not turn work.

With right hand tip of needle, pick up and k 4 sts evenly spaced across the long side of piece, then pick up and k 3 sts across cast-on edge of piece—10 sts on needle.

Set-Up Rows

Row 1 K3, place marker (pm), p4, pm, k3.

Row 2 K to marker, slip marker (sm), *k1, yo; rep from * to next marker, sm, k to end of row—14 sts.

Section I

Row 1 (WS) K to marker, sm, p to next marker, sm, k to end of row.

Easy Half-Circle Shawl

Row 2 Knit, slipping markers as you come to them.

Row 3 Rep Row 1.

Row 4 (Increase Row) K to marker, sm, *yo, k1; rep from * to next marker, sm, k to end of row—22 sts.

As you work the following sections, continue to slip the markers as you come to them.

Section II

Rows 1 and 3 (WS) K to marker, p to next marker, k to end of row.

Rows 2 and 4 Knit.

Row 5 Knit.

Row 6 (Increase Row) K3, *k1, yo; rep from * to next marker, k to end of row—38 sts.

Section III

Row 1 (WS) Knit.

Rows 2, 4, 6, 8 and 10 Knit.

Rows 3, 5, 7, and 9 K to marker, p to next marker, k to end of row.

Row 11 Knit.

Row 12 (Increase Row) K3, *yo, k1; rep from * to next marker, k to end of row—70 sts.

Section IV

Row 1 (WS) Knit.

Row 2 and all even numbered rows to Row 22 Knit.

Row 3 and all odd numbered rows to Row 21 K to marker, p to next marker, k to end of row.

Row 23 Knit.

Row 24 (Increase Row) K3, *k1, yo; rep from * to next marker, k to end of row—134 sts.

Section V

Row 1 (WS) Knit.

Row 2 and all even numbered rows to Row 46 Knit.

Row 3 and all odd numbered rows to Row 45 K to marker, p to next marker, k to end of row.

Row 47 Knit.

Row 48 (Increase Row) K3, *yo, k1; rep from * to next marker, k to end of row—262 sts.

Section VI

Row 1 (WS) Knit.

Row 2 and all even numbered rows to Row 16 Knit.

Row 3 and all odd numbered rows to Row 15 K to marker, p to next marker, k to end of row.

Rows 17–26 Knit.

Bind off as follows:

Step 1 K2, insert the left hand needle into the front of the 2 sts you just worked (that are on the right hand needle), wrap the yarn around right needle and knit 2 together through back loop—1 st on right hand needle.

Step 2 Knit next st from left hand needle, then insert the left hand needle into the front of the 2 sts and knit 2 together through back loop—1 st on right hand needle.

Rep Step 2 until you have just 1 st on right hand needle.

Cut yarn and fasten off last st.

FINISHING

Blocking

Dampen Shawl thoroughly. Spread a towel onto a flat surface, then lay Shawl onto towel and smooth into shape. Gently shape Shawl to match finished measurements. Use blocking wires if desired to further shape Shawl. Allow to air dry.

Weave in ends. •

Thick and Quick Mittens

●●
Easy

MEASUREMENTS
One size to fit most women
Circumference 8"/20.5cm
Length Approx 10½"/26.5cm

MATERIALS
Yarn
LION BRAND® *Heartland*®, *Thick & Quick*®, 5oz/142g skeins; each 125yd/114m (acrylic)
• 1 skein in #113 Redwood

Needles
• One pair size 9 (5.5mm) knitting needles, *or size to obtain gauge*
• One pair size 10 (6mm) knitting needles, *or size to obtain gauge*

Notions
• Stitch markers
• Stitch holders
• Tapestry needle

GAUGE
13 sts + 19 rows = 4"/10cm in St st (k on RS, p on WS), using size 10 (6mm) needles. *BE SURE TO CHECK YOUR GAUGE.*

NOTES
1) Mittens are worked flat beginning at cuff and then seamed.
2) Smaller needles are used for the ribbed cuff of the Mittens to create a snug fit.
3) The hand portion of the Mitten is worked in Stockinette stitch, increasing sts to make the thumb gusset, and decreasing stitches to shape the top of the Mitten.
4) The sts for the thumb are placed onto a holder, then the thumb is worked after you finish making the hand portion of the Mitten.
5) Mittens are worked at a tight gauge so that they are dense and long wearing.

MITTENS (MAKE 2)
Ribbed Cuff
With smaller needles and leaving a long yarn tail, cast on 26 sts.
Row 1 (RS) *K2, p2, rep from * to last 2 sts, k2.
Row 2 *P2, k2, rep from * to last 2 sts, p2.
Rows 3–8 Rep Rows 1 and 2.

Begin Hand
Change to larger needles as you work the next row.
Next Row K13, M1, k to end of row. At the end of this row, you will have 27 sts.
Beginning with a WS (purl) row, work in St st for 5 rows.

Shape Thumb Gusset
Row 1 (RS) K13, pm, M1, k1, M1, pm, k to end of row. At the end of Row 1 you will have 29 sts.
Row 2 and all WS rows Purl.
Row 3 K to marker, sm, M1, k to next marker, M1, sm, k to end of row. Every time you work Row 3, you will be increasing 2 sts to make the thumb gusset.
Rep Rows 2 and 3 until you have 11 sts between markers.
Purl 1 row.

Shape Mitten
Next Row K to marker, remove marker, slip next 11 sts to a st holder, remove next marker, k to end of row.
Beginning with a WS (purl) row, continue in St st on the 26 sts that remain on your needle for approx 4"/10cm past the st holder, end with a RS (knit) row as the last row you work.
Next Row (WS) P13, place marker, p to end of row.

Shape Top of Mitten
Row 1 (RS) K1, ssk, k to 3 sts before marker, k2tog, k1, sm, k1, ssk, k to last 3 sts, k2tog, k1—you will have 22 sts.
Row 2 Purl.

42

Rep last 2 rows for 3 more times—you will have 10 sts.

Next Row K1, ssk, k2, remove marker, k2, k2tog, k1—you will have 8 sts.

Next Row Purl.

Cut yarn, leaving a long yarn tail. Thread yarn tail into blunt needle. Beginning with last st on (knitting) needle, draw blunt needle through remaining sts. Pull to gather sts together and fasten off.

Thumb

Slip 11 sts for thumb from holder back onto larger needle so that you are ready to work a RS (knit) row. Join yarn, leaving a long yarn tail, and k across.

Continue in St st for 5 more rows.

Next row K1, (ssk) twice, k1, (k2tog) twice, k1.

Cut yarn, leaving a long yarn tail. Thread yarn tail into blunt needle. Beginning with last st on (knitting) needle, draw blunt needle through remaining sts. Pull to gather sts together and fasten off.

FINISHING

Thread beginning yarn tail into blunt needle and seam sides of Mitten. Thread yarn tail at thumb into blunt needle and seam hole at base of thumb and sides of thumb. Weave in ends. •

Cheltenham Hat

Easy

MEASUREMENTS
Circumference Approx 19"/48.5cm
Height Approx 9"/23cm
Note Hat will stretch to fit a range of sizes.

MATERIALS
Yarn
LION BRAND® *Go For Faux*®, 3½ oz/100g skeins; each 64yd/60m (polyester) **6**
• 1 skein in #204 Chinchilla

Needles
• One set (5) double-pointed needles (dpn) size 10½ (6.5mm), *or size to obtain gauge*

Notions
• Tapestry needle

GAUGE
10½ sts = 4"/10cm over pattern, using size 10½ (6.5mm) dpn.
BE SURE TO CHECK YOUR GAUGE.

NOTES
1) The Hat is knit in one piece in the round.
2) You'll be knitting in the round on double-pointed needles, but unlike traditional knitting in the round, you do not need to place a marker for the beginning of the round. Due to the nature of this yarn, it won't show if you stop knitting at any point in a round.

HAT
Cast on 50 sts—with 12 sts on each of 2 needles and 13 sts on each of 2 needles.
Join by knitting the first st on the left-hand needle with the working yarn from the right-hand needle.
K every rnd until you have approx 2yd/2m of yarn rem.
Last Rnd K2tog around—25 sts.
Cut yarn, leaving a long yarn tail. Thread yarn tail into blunt needle, then draw needle through remaining sts. Pull to gather top of Hat and knot securely.

FINISHING
Weave in yarn ends. •

Diagonal Knit Scarf

Easy

MEASUREMENTS
Approx 8"/20.5cm x 60"/152.5cm

MATERIALS
Yarn

LION BRAND® *Scarfie®*, 5.3oz/150g skeins; each 312yd/285m
(acrylic, wool) (5)
• 1 skein in #201 Cream/Black

Needles
• One pair size 11 (8mm) knitting needles, *or size to obtain gauge*

Notion
• Tapestry needle

GAUGE
12 sts = 4"/10cm over Rows 1–6 of pattern, using size 11 (8mm)
needles. *BE SURE TO CHECK YOUR GAUGE.*

NOTES
1) Scarf is worked in one piece.
2) The first section of the Scarf is shaped with increases and the last
section is shaped with decreases.
3) The increases and decreases create a diagonal pattern on the
Scarf.

SCARF
Cast on 3 sts.

First Section
Row 1 Kfb, k to end of row—you will have 4 sts at the end of Row 1.
Rep Row 1 until you have 36 sts.

Center Section
Row 1 Kfb, k to end of row.
Row 2 K2tog, k to end of row.
Rep Rows 1 and 2 until longer side edge measures approx
60"/152.5cm, end with a Row 2 as the last row you work.

Last Section
Row 1 K2tog, k to end of row—you will have 35 sts.
Rep Row 1 until you have only 3 sts rem.
Bind off.

FINISHING
Weave in ends. •

Simple Cabled Hat

● ● ●
Intermediate

MEASUREMENTS
Circumference Approx 20"/51cm
Length 9"/23 cm
Note Hat will stretch to fit a range of head sizes.

MATERIALS
Yarn
LION BRAND® *Heartland*®, *Thick & Quick*® 5oz/142g skeins; each
125yd/114m (acrylic)
• 1 skein in #151 Katmai

Needles
• One set (5) double-pointed needles (dpn) size 11 (8mm), *or size to obtain gauge*

Notions
• Cable needle
• Stitch marker
• Tapestry needle

GAUGE
• 12 sts + 16 rows = 4"/10cm over pattern Rows 1–16 using size 11 (8mm) dpn. *BE SURE TO CHECK YOUR GAUGE.*

STITCH GLOSSARY
2/2 LC (2 over 2 left cross) Sl 2 sts to cable needle and hold in front of work, k2, then k2 from cable needle.
2/2 RC (2 over 2 right cross) Sl 2 sts to cable needle and hold in back of work, k2, then k2 from cable needle.

NOTES
1) Hat is worked in the round on double-pointed needles (dpn).
2) Simple cables are worked on the body of the Hat. Decreases to shape the top of the Hat are incorporated into the cables.

HAT
Cast on 60 sts. Divide sts onto 4 needles, with 15 sts on each needle. Pm for beg of rnd. Join by working the first st on the left-hand needle with the working yarn from the right-hand needle and being careful not to twist sts.
Rnds 1–3 *P2, k4; rep from * around.
Rnd 4 *P2, 2/2 LC, p2, 2/2 RC; rep from * around.

Rnds 5–20 Rep Rnds 1–4.
Rnds 21–23 Rep Rnds 1–3.

Shape Crown (top of Hat)
Rnd 24 *P2, sl next 2 sts to cable needle and hold in front of work, k2tog, then k2 from cable needle, p2, sl next 2 sts to cable needle and hold in back of work, k2, then k2tog from cable needle; rep from * around—50 sts at the end of this rnd.
Rnd 25 *P2, k3; rep from * around.
Rnd 26 *P2, sl next st to cable needle and hold in front of work, k2tog, then k1 from cable needle, p2, sl next st to cable needle and hold in back of work, k2tog, then k1 from cable needle; rep from * around—40 sts.
Rnd 27 *P2, k2; rep from * around.
Rnd 28 P2, sl next st to cable needle and hold in front of work, k1, then k1 from cable needle, p2, sl next st to cable needle and hold in back of work, k1, then k1 from cable needle; rep from * around.
Rnd 29 Rep Rnd 27.
Rnd 30 P2tog, sl next st to cable needle and hold in front of work, k1, then k1 from cable needle, p2tog, sl next st to cable needle and hold in back of work, k1, then k1 from cable needle; rep from * around—30 sts.
Rnd 31 *P1, k2; rep from * around.
Rnd 32 *P1, ssk, p1, k2tog; rep from * around—20 sts.
Rnd 33 *P1, k1; rep from * around.
Rnd 34 K2tog around—10 sts.
Rnd 35 Knit.
Rnd 36 *K2tog, k1, k2tog, k1, k2tog, k2tog—6 sts.
Cut yarn, leaving a long yarn tail. Thread yarn tail through remaining sts and pull to gather. Knot securely.

FINISHING
Weave in ends.●

Cabled Bun Hat

Easy

MEASUREMENTS
Circumference Approx 20"/51cm
Height Approx 6"/15cm
Note Hat will stretch to fit a range of sizes.

MATERIALS
Yarn
LION BRAND® *Scarfie*®, 5.3oz/150g skeins; each 312yd/285m (acrylic, wool) 5
• 1 skein in #216 Cream/Silver

Needles
• One pair size 7 (4.5mm) knitting needles, *or size to obtain gauge*
• One set (5) double-pointed needles (dpn) size 7 (4.5mm), *or size to obtain gauge*

Notions
• Cable needle
• Tapestry needle

GAUGE
32 sts = 4"/10cm over Rows 1-4 of pattern. *BE SURE TO CHECK YOUR GAUGE.*

STITCH GLOSSARY
2/2 LC (2 over 2 left cross) Sl 2 sts to cable needle and hold in front, k2, then k2 from cable needle.
RT (Right Twist) K2tog and leave on left-hand needle, then with right-hand needle, go between the 2 sts and k the first st again.

NOTES
1) Hat is worked in one piece and then seamed.
2) The top of the Hat is open.
3) Yarn overs are worked every 4 rows to create eyelets. A knitted cord is worked separately, then woven through the eyelets to shape the top of the Hat.

HAT
With straight needles, cast on 48 sts.
Rows 1 and 3 (WS) K2, *p4, k2, p2, k2; rep from * to last 6 sts, p4, k2.

Row 2 K1, p1, *k4, p2, RT, p2; rep from * to last 6 sts, k4, p1, k1.
Row 4 K1, p1, *2/2 LC, p2, RT, p2; rep from * to last 16 sts, 2/2 LC, p2, RT, yo, p2tog, 2/2 LC, p1, k1.

Rep Rows 1–4 until piece measures approx 20"/51cm from beginning, end with a Row 2 as the last row you work.
Bind off.

FINISHING
Sew ends of piece together to make a ring.

Knitted Cord
With 2 dpn, cast on 3 sts. Knit the 3 sts. Do not turn work. *Slide sts to other end of needle and knit them, pulling yarn tightly across the back of the work, (do not turn work); rep from * until cord measures approx 31"/78.5cm long.
Bind off.
Weave cord through the yarn over eyelets, then knot ends of cord together.
Weave in ends. •

Checkerboard Rib Scarf

Easy

MEASUREMENTS
Approx 9"/23cm x 36"/91.5cm

MATERIALS
Yarn
LION BRAND® *Scarfie®*, 5.3oz/150g skeins; each 312yd/285m (acrylic, wool) **⑤**
• 1 skein in #206 Cream/Taupe

Needles
• One pair size 8 (5mm) knitting needles, *or size to obtain gauge*

Notion
• Tapestry needle

GAUGE
20 sts = 4"/10cm in checkerboard rib pattern, using size 8 (5mm) needles. *BE SURE TO CHECK YOUR GAUGE.*

NOTE
Scarf is knit in one piece in an easy knit and purl pattern.

SCARF
Work in checkerboard rib pattern as follows:

Row 1 (RS) *K11, p2, k2, p2, k1; rep from * once more, k10.
Row 2 (WS) P1, *k8, p2, (k2, p2) twice; rep from * once more, k8, p1.
Row 3 K1, *p8, (k2, p2) twice, k2; rep from * once more, p8, k1.
Row 4 P10, *p1, k2, p2, k2, p11; rep from * once more.
Rows 5-8 Rep Rows 1–4.
Row 9 Knit.
Row 10 (P2, k2) twice, *p12, k2, p2, k2; rep from * once more, p2.
Row 11 *(K2, p2) twice, k2, p8; rep from * once more, (k2, p2) twice, k2.
Row 12 (P2, k2) twice, p2, *k8, (p2, k2) twice, p2; rep from * once more.
Row 13 (K2, p2) twice, *k12, p2, k2, p2; rep from * once more, k2.
Rows 14–17 Rep Rows 10-13.
Row 18 Purl.

Rep Rows 1–18 for 12 more times, then rep Rows 1–8 once more. Bind off as if to knit.

FINISHING
Weave in ends. •

Hat and Scarf Set

●●
Easy

MEASUREMENTS

Hat
Circumference Approx 21"/53.5cm,
Note Hat will stretch to fit a range of sizes.
Scarf
Approx 8½"/21.5cm x 34"/86.5cm

MATERIALS

Yarn
LION BRAND® *Mandala*®, 5.3oz/150g skeins; each 590yd/540m (acrylic)
• 1 skein in #214 Centaur

Needles
• One pair size 6 (4mm) knitting needles, *or size to obtain gauge.*
• One pair size 8 (5mm) knitting needles, *or size to obtain gauge.*

Notions
• Stitch markers
• Tapestry needle

GAUGE

19 sts + 24 rows = 4"/10cm in St st (k on RS, p on WS). *BE SURE TO CHECK YOUR GAUGE.*

NOTES

1) Hat is worked in one piece and then seamed.
2) Scarf is worked in one piece, then ends are seamed. The seamed ends allow for styling options.

HAT

With larger needles, cast on 100 sts.
Work in St st for 10 rows.
Change to smaller needles.
Row 1 (RS) K1, *k4, p3; rep from * to last st, k1.
Row 2 K1, *k3, p4; rep from * to last st, k1.
Rows 3–8 Rep Rows 1 and 2.
Knit 6 rows, then rep Rows 1–8 once more.
Work in St st until piece measures approx 10"/25.5cm from beg, end with a WS row.

Shape Top of Hat
Row 1 (RS) K1, *pm, k2tog, k12; rep from * to last st, k1.
Row 2 Purl.
Row 3 K1, *sm, k2tog, knit to next marker; rep from * to last st, k1.
Row 4 Purl.
Rep the last 2 rows until you have 23 sts.
Last Row (RS) K1, (k3tog) 7 times, k1—9 sts.
Cut yarn, leaving a long yarn tail. Thread yarn tail into blunt needle, then draw through rem sts. Pull to close top of Hat, then knot.

FINISHING

Sew sides of piece to make Hat.
Weave in ends.

SCARF

With larger needles, cast on 40 sts.
Work in St st for 10 rows.
Row 1 (RS) K1, *k3, p4; rep from * to last 4 sts, k4.
Row 2 K1, purl to last st, k1.
Rep Rows 1 and 2 until piece measures approx 33"/84cm from beg.
Work in St st for 10 rows.
Bind off.

FINISHING

Fold sides at one end of Scarf in to meet at center of Scarf. Seam ends tog for approx 4"/10cm.
Rep on opposite end of Scarf.
Weave in ends. •

Howell Cowl

Easy

MEASUREMENTS
Circumference Approx 22"/56cm
Height Approx 10"/25.5cm

MATERIALS
Yarn
LION BRAND® *Vanna's Choice*®, 3½oz/100g skeins, each
170yd/156m (acrylic, rayon) ⓸
• 1 skein in #133 Brick

Needle
• One size 6 (4mm) circular needle, 16"/40.5cm long, *or size to
obtain gauge*

Notions
• Stitch markers
• Tapestry needle

GAUGE
12 sts = 4"/10cm over Rnds 1 and 2 of pattern, using size 6 (4mm)
needle. *BE SURE TO CHECK YOUR GAUGE.*

NOTES
1) Cowl is worked in one piece in the round on a circular needle.
2) The pattern stitch used creates a very stretchy Cowl!

COWL
Loosely cast on 64 sts.
Pm for beg of rnd and join by working the first st on the left-hand
needle with the working yarn from the right-hand needle. Sm as
you come to it at the beg of each rnd.
Rnd 1 Purl.
Rnd 2 *P 1, k the next st in the row below (to k in the row below,
insert your needle into the st below the next st on your left-hand
needle, then complete the st as a usual knit st); rep from * around.
Rep Rnds 1 and 2 until piece measures approx 10"/25.5cm from
beg, end with a Rnd 1 as the last rnd you work.
Bind off loosely. (**Tip** An easy way to bind off loosely is to simply use
a needle one size larger.)

FINISHING
Weave in ends. •

Snowball Hat

Easy

MEASUREMENTS
Circumference Approx 7½"/44.5cm
Length Approx 8"/20.5cm
Note Hat will stretch to fit a range of sizes.

MATERIALS
Yarn
LION BRAND® *Wool-Ease®*, *Thick & Quick®*, 6oz/170g skeins; each 106yd/97m (acrylic, wool) **(6)**
• 1 skein in #099 Fisherman

Needles
• One set (5) double-pointed needles (dpn) size 15 (10mm), *or size to obtain gauge*

Notions
• Stitch markers
• Pom-pom maker
• Tapestry needle

GAUGE
10 sts = 4"/10cm over Rnd 1 of pattern, using size 15 (10mm) dpn.
BE SURE TO CHECK YOUR GAUGE.

NOTES
1) Hat is worked in one piece in the round on double-pointed needles (dpn).
2) Pom-pom is tied to the top of the finished Hat.

HAT
Loosely cast on 44 sts. Divide sts onto 4 needles, with 11 sts on each needle.
Pm for beg of rnd and join by working the first st on the left-hand needle with the working yarn from the right-hand needle and being careful not to twist sts.

Rnd 1 *K1, p1; rep from * around.
Rep Rnd 1 until piece measures approx 7"/18cm from beg.

Shape Crown (top of Hat)
Next Rnd K2tog around—you'll have 22 sts.
Next Rnd K2tog around—you'll have 11 sts.

Next Rnd Knit the first st, then k2tog around—you'll have 6 sts.
Cut yarn, leaving a long yarn tail. Thread yarn tail into blunt needle, then draw through rem 6 sts and pull to close the top of Hat.
Knot securely.

FINISHING
Following pom-pom maker directions, make a large pom-pom and tie to top of Hat.
Weave in yarn ends. •

Huldra Hat

Easy

MEASUREMENTS

Circumference Approx 19"/48.5cm

Note Hat will stretch to fit a range of sizes.

MATERIALS

Yarn

LION BRAND® *Scarfie®*, 5.3oz/150g skeins; each 312yd/285m (acrylic, wool) **(5)**

• 1 skein in #201 Cream/Black

Needles

• One size 8 (5mm) circular needle, 16"/40.5cm long, 16"/40.5cm long, *or size to obtain gauge*

• One set (5) double-pointed needles (dpn) size 8 (5mm), *or size to obtain gauge*

Notions

• Stitch markers

• Tapestry needle

• 3"/7.5cm square piece of cardboard

GAUGE

18 sts = 4"/10cm in St st worked in rnds (k every st on every rnd).
BE SURE TO CHECK YOUR GAUGE.

STITCH GLOSSARY

Cable Cast-On *Insert right needle between first 2 sts on left needle, wrap yarn and pull through (as if knitting a st), transfer new st to left needle; rep from * for desired number of sts.

NOTES

1) Earflaps are worked first, then stitches are cast on between Earflaps for the back of Hat.

2) Lower back of Hat is worked in rows then stitches are cast on for front of Hat and work is joined to work in the round.

3) Decreases are worked to shape top of Hat. When stitches have been sufficiently decreased, double pointed needles are used instead of the circular needle.

4) Stitches are picked up on lower edge of each Earflap for the cords.

5) Tassels are tied to the end of each cord and to the top of the Hat.

HAT

First Earflap

With dpn, cast on 4 sts. Work back and forth in rows using 2 dpns.

Row 1 (WS) Purl.

Row 2 (Increase Row) K1, M1, k to last st, M1, k1—6 sts.

Rows 3–14 Rep Rows 1 and 2 for 6 more times—you will have 18 sts in Row 14.

Row 15 Purl.

Cut yarn, leaving sts on one dpn, and set aside.

Second Earflap

Cast on and make same as First Earflap, but do not cut yarn.

Cast On for Back of Hat

From RS, with circular needle and yarn still attached to Second Earflap, k across sts of Second Earflap; turn, cable cast on 21 sts for back of Hat, turn; with same yarn, k across sts of First Earflap—you will have 57 sts.

Next Row (WS) K17, k2tog, k19, k2tog, k to end of row—55 sts.
Beg with a RS (knit) row, work in St st (k on RS, p on WS) for 4 rows.

Cast On for Front of Hat and Join

Next Rnd (RS) Cable cast on 30 sts for front of Hat; beg over sts just cast on, k29, k2tog, k16, k2tog, k17, k2tog, k to last st, being careful not to twist sts, knit the last st together with the first cast-on st—81 sts.
Place marker for beg of rnd.
Work in St st worked in rnds (k every st on every rnd) until Hat measures about 8½"/21.5cm measured from cast-on sts at front.

Shape Top of Hat

Note Change from circular needle to dpn when sts have been sufficiently deceased.

Rnd 1 *K25, k2tog; rep from * 2 more times—78 sts.

Rnd 2 Knit.

Rnd 3 (Dec Rnd) (K11, k2tog) 6 times—72 sts.

Rnd 4 Knit.

Rnd 5 (Dec Rnd) (K10, k2tog) 6 times—66 sts.

Rnd 6 (Dec Rnd) (K9, k2tog) 6 times—60 sts.

Rnd 7 (Dec Rnd) (K8, k2tog) 6 times—54 sts.

Rnd 8 (Dec Rnd) (K7, k2tog) 6 times—48 sts.

Rnd 9 (Dec Rnd) (K6, k2tog) 6 times—42 sts.
Rnd 10 (Dec Rnd) (K5, k2tog) 6 times—36 sts.
Rnd 11 (Dec Rnd) (K4, k2tog) 6 times—30 sts.
Rnd 12 (Dec Rnd) (K3, k2tog) 6 times—24 sts.
Rnd 13 (Dec Rnd) (K2, k2tog) 6 times—18 sts.
Rnd 14 (Dec Rnd) (K1, k2tog) 6 times—12 sts.
Rnd 15 (Dec Rnd) K2tog around—6 sts.
Cut yarn, leaving a long yarn tail. Thread yarn
tail into blunt needle, then draw through rem
sts. Pull tail to close opening at top of Hat.
Knot securely.

FINISHING

Cords

From RS with dpn, pick up and k4 sts evenly
spaced across cast-on edge of First Earflap.
Knit the 4 sts. Do not turn work. *Slide sts to
other end of needle and knit them, pulling
yarn tightly across the back of the work, (do
not turn work); rep from * until cord measures
about 4½"/11.5cm or desired length.
Last Row (K2tog) twice.
Cut yarn, leaving a long yarn tail. Thread yarn
tail into blunt needle, then draw through rem
2 sts. Knot securely.
Rep to make a cord on Second Earflap.

Tassels (make 3)

Wrap yarn around 3"/7.5cm cardboard about
23 times. Cut a 12"/30.5cm length of yarn
and thread, doubled, into large-eyed blunt
needle. Insert needle under all strands at
upper edge of cardboard. Pull tightly and
knot securely near strands. Cut yarn loops at
lower edge of cardboard. Cut a 10"/25.5cm
length of yarn and wrap tightly around loops
about ¾"/2cm below top knot to form tassel
neck. Knot securely; thread ends onto needle
and weave ends to center of tassel.
Trim tassel ends evenly.
Tie a tassel to the end of each cord and to
top of Hat.
Weave in ends. •

Lina Tied Scarf

Easy

MEASUREMENTS
Approx 13"/33cm x 48"/122cm, at longest and widest points

MATERIALS
Yarn

LION BRAND® *Vel-Luxe*®, 5.3oz/150g skeins; each 246yd/225m (polyester) **(4)**
• 1 skein in #150 Charcoal

Needles
• One pair size 7 (4.5mm) knitting needles, *or size to obtain gauge*

Notions
• Stitch markers
• Tapestry needle

GAUGE
20 sts = 4"/10cm over Garter st (knit every st on every row), using size 7 (4.5mm) needles. *BE SURE TO CHECK YOUR GAUGE.*

NOTES
1) The tie is worked first, then stitches are picked up along the tie to make the Scarf.
2) The Scarf and tie are both worked in Garter stitch.

TIE
Cast on 9 sts.
Work in Garter st until piece measures approx 48"/122cm from beg. Bind off.

SCARF
Fold tie in half to find the center, then place a marker on the center. Place 2 more markers on tie, each 8"/20.5cm from center marker.
Note Since tie was worked in Garter st (a reversible st), there isn't a right or wrong side. Just choose one side of the tie to be the RS. From chosen RS, and beginning at outside st marker, pick up and knit 40 sts evenly spaced from outside marker to center maker, pick up and knit one st at center marker, then 40 sts evenly spaced from center marker to second outside marker—total of 81 sts on your needle.
Remove markers.
Row 1 (WS) Knit.

Row 2 (Dec Row) K2, k2tog, knit to end of row.
Rep Row 2 until you have 4 sts remaining.
Next Row K2, k2tog—3 sts.
Next Row Slip 1, k2tog, pass slip st over.
Fasten off last st.

FINISHING
Weave in ends. •